Miss Passport City Guides Presents:

Mini 3 day Unforgettable Vacation Itinerary to Frankfurt, Germany

Sharon Bell

Miss Passport City Guides Presents:
Mini 3 day Unforgettable Vacation Itinerary to
Frankfurt, Germany

By Sharon Bell
© 2014 Mini Trips Publishing,LLC
Duplication prohibited

From the Desk James Moore Editor of Bull City Publishing:

Dear Friend,

If at Any point while you're reading this book you have any questions, please don't hesitate to contact us. You can best reach us at Twitter (@bullcitypub), or on our Facebook Fan Page

Even if you don't have any questions, We'd love for you to come by and say hello! If you want to reach us in a private you can email us at info@bullcitypublishing.com or on our blog Bullcitypublishing.com/blog

Warmest Regards,

James Moore

EDITOR & CHIEF ,BULL CITY PUBLISHING, LLC

Do you Love Reading? Do you Want a Ton of FREE Kindle Books? Join our Mailing list by Emailing us at freebooks@bullcitypublishing.com

.

CONTENTS

MINI 3 DAY UNFORGETTABLE VACATION ITINERARY TO FRANKFURT, GERMANY

If I could travel anywhere in the world, I would have to say I would want it to be Frankfurt Germany. Day 1, I started my first day site seeing and visiting historical landmarks. Witnessing first hand a new culture, surrounded by a new group of people experiencing different languages, different but delightful food dishes, clothes, and religion, wow that's amazing. The typical adventure travelers were adults, young, single, employed, and other tourist. They enjoy adventurous traveling as myself; white water rafting, bungee jumping, bike tours, and wild like tours, they are the travelers that go when and where they please. As I travel throughout the city, I would bet that the increase in leisure travel can be equated by personal lifestyles, past experiences, perception of life, personal circumstances and child or health changes.

Even the history of Frankfurt, Germany is appealing; what appeared to be the motivation for travel can be equated on personal satisfaction and reward to some. Others felt the psychological aspect of being in different environment brought about great pleasure. The value of money, accommodations, and convenience played a vast change for travel to their destination. Being able to travel enables individuals to achieve their goals related to tourism through compliance, structuring, and practices. Its importance is centered on infrastructural, social tourism, growth, and sustainability; without it there would be no structure or guidelines for tourism.

Something that was quite unique about Frankfurt, that historically even though most of it was destroyed in World War II, and rebuilt in a modern style, it still looks as if it could be a historical site that's been around for centuries. Frankfurt Am Main translates to Frankfurt on the river and in the mid-19th- century was the capital of Germany. Frankfurt Germany was an industrial city that was a prime target forAllied bombing during the war. The bombing on Frankfurt began as early as July 1941, during a continuous and relentless British air raid against the Nazis. In March 1944, Frankfurt suffered extraordinary damage during a raid that saw 27,000 tons of bombs dropped on Germany in just a single month. Consequently, Frankfurt's Medieval Old Town was practically completely destroyed.

Through a devastating past, of the near nnihilation of Frankfurt Germany and the almost successful genocide of the Jewish people, Frankfurt Germany managed to thrive into today's time and still maintain its colorful history and culture.

Day two was spent enjoying the tour of the Römer, it's been around for about six centuries, in

1405, the city council purchased the buildings at the Römer from the merchant Kunz for 800 guldens of good (Frankfurt currency in cash). The Römer has bear witness to elections and coronation of German rulers. Until 1846, the Römer halls in the middle building served as halls for markets and fairs but Frankfurt's town hall suffered serious damage in the Second World War. Luckily, like the rest of the city the Römer was renovated and repaired and now stands as undoubtedly the most famous landmark of Frankfurt Germany.

Something else that would be exciting to see in Frankfurt Germany is all the different ways that religion has shaped and molded the city. In America you see signs of our religion everywhere. Religious travelers often travel to satisfy their religious beliefs and covenant; fulfilling one's curiosity in their faith and practices of worship.

On our money, "In God we Trust", in our pledge of allegiance, "One nation under god for which it stands". Tourist dollar is so valuable to its competition, it help government realize that tourism brings about additional revenue. Increase value of the euro against the U.S. dollar lead to fewer American traveling broad until the dollar improves. The not so attractive side of tourism is taxation, skilled level employees jobless, business are closing. Government are bring outside people that are more skilled to work. Good and services from local residents are being outsourced, while more goods are imported.

Later that day we visited a 95 m high tower rising over Frankfurt Germany, that dates all the way back to the year 852, called the Cathedral, over time ten emperors were crowned there between 1562 and 1792. With a history that dates back to 852 reaching a height that can be seen nearly throughout the city. The Cathedral alone must have had a large impact on Frankfurt, and the people inhabiting it. I could only begin to imagine the influence of religion as a whole in Frankfurt Germany.

Beyond Frankfurt Germany's long history and the impact of its religious surrounding, Frankfurt Germany has smaller cultural differences. Things as simple as the greetings in this culture, like the handshake for example, is done slightly different in Germany than in America. The man is to wait until the woman puts her hand out before shaking it, and also crossing someone else's handshake is inappropriate. Some things in this culture like chewing gum in public is seen as inappropriate; talking with your hands in your pockets is disrespectful; and instead of crossing the fingers for good luck they simply squeeze their thumb.

The dating in Germany is different than in the United States, instead of the man paying for dinner, they each pay for their own food and entertainment unless it is a special occasion. Frankfurt Germany will be a place of new experiences, new sites to see, and a fascinating new place to be. Rich cultural experience, for a day of leisure tourist may enjoy mountain climbing, artwork and religious figures in rich collections in museums and libraries, historical festivities and agricultural events, site seeing and food from all cultural cuisines where all dishes are delightful and plentiful. As with other cities tourist too have to view deteriorating economic conditions led to recurrent violence of rival's gangs affiliated with the major political parties evolved into powerful organized crime networks involved in international drug smuggling and money laundering. Violent crimes drug tracking, and poverty pose significant challenges to the government today. Where ever the next destination, we the tourist overlook other unpleasant sides of traveling because we are the travelers that go when and where we please despite the economic conditions of a vacation site. Nonetheless, many rural and resort area remain relatively safe and contribute substantially to the economy, even Germany it wouldn't be impossible to notice no overcrowding and polluted beaches, no overcrowding cities, high crime rates, depletion of fish stocks, exotic plants, animals, and wildlife, water pollution, defamation of cultural and ecological tourist sites although I know in some parts of Germany it too exists, still just pure beauty!

Tourism policy is structured also in Germany its decision making strategy help enables individuals to achieve their goals related to tourism through compliance, structuring, and practices. It's important is centered on infrastructural, social tourism, growth, and sustainability; without it there would be no structure or guidelines for tourism. Various groups all share a common goal in development of tourism and need to be involved in decision- making policy information to ensure success. World Tourism Organization set out to accomplish their mission even in Frankfurt Germany such as to develop and practice protection policies for economic sustainability. Its purpose is to mandate policies as a whole for all tourist industries, it also provides vital information on issues and concerns for its members and agencies. They cooperate because they share the same common goal which is to increase tourist experience. The organization acts as an information resource center by promoting safety, security, and technical standards. Many nations see tourism as a panacea to provide economic quick fix to ease a loss of production, employment, or revenues. Many feel that the government should assume the lead role in the tourism industry and its economic policy. Various groups all share a common goal in development of tourism and need to be involved in decision- making policy information to ensure success. Their mission is to develop and practice protection policies for economic growth, job creation, international trade while fostering peace and respect to human rights, cultural and political awareness. Its purpose is to mandate policies as a whole for all tourist industries, it also provides vital information on issues and concerns for its members and agencies. They should cooperate because they share the same common goal which is to increase tourist experience.

Day three, Time here stretches; my time in Germany, and a short seven days, was almost up. My last day was spent enjoying a jazz festival event, an attraction filled with concerts, musicals of all types as well as comedy shows. These are more likely to satisfy my level of human need and self-actualization. As I sat listening to sounds of great music in a lively port area, no cars, buses or transportation of any kind, I then began to imagine and see beautiful images trees, color of the land and sea, pink, yellow , violet, flowers and romance painting of the earth so beautifully. For moments I was taken away to the sweet smell of beauty and striking abundance of joy and excitement that I didn't want to end. My week long vacation was coming to an end. As I sipped a glass of red wine, the music of different artist began to arouse my sense of happiness. I soon felt realization began to settle in, things here are resemblance of what life should always be filled with family, love, happiness, joy, food and fun. No need to be transported, back home the landscape tells it all right here in Frankfurt Germany, hopefully this journey will someday unfold to reality.

WORK CITED

http://www.history.com/this-day-in-history/patton-takes-frankfurt

http://www.frankfurt.de/sixcms/detail.php?id=468 81&template=bildanzeige

http://www.frankfurt.de/sixcms/detail.php?id=317 578&_ffmpar[_id_inhalt]=5021019

http://www.everyculture.com/Ge-It/Germany.html

http://www.frankfurt.de/sixcms/detail.php?id=stadt frankfurt_eval01.c.125161.en

http://www.east-buc.k12.ia.us/02_03/cul/germany/germany.htm

OTHER AMAZING MINI TRAVEL GUIDES FROM THE MISS PASSPORT TRAVEL GUIDE SERIES

Thank You for Your Purchase!!!!!

Thank you again for Ordering this book!

I hope this book was able to provide you with the Information that you were searching for. Lastly, if you REALLY enjoyed this book, then I'd like to ask you for a favor, would you be kind enough to leave a review for this book on Amazon? It'd be greatly appreciated!

Lastly, Please Besure to connect with us We Would Love to Hear from You

Bull City Publishing Social Media Links:

Blog: http://bullcitypublishing.com/blog/

Facebook Group:
https://www.facebook.com/groups/bullcitypublishing/

Twitter : https://twitter.com/BullCityPub

Instagram: http://instagram.com/bullcitypublishing

Pintrest: https://pintrest.com/bullcitypub

Linkedin:
http://www.linkedin.com/companies/5311112

Tumblr: http://bullcitypublishing.tumblr.com

Do you Love Reading? Do you Want a Ton of FREE Kindle Books? Join our Mailing list by Emailing us at freebooks@bullcitypublishing.com

Do you Need Help Writing a Book? Would you like to get published? If So Shoot us an email publish@bullcitypublishing.com

Thank you and good luck!

James Moore

15585731R10015

Printed in Great Britain
by Amazon